Workbook for Dan Sullivan & Benjamin Hardy's ***10x Is Easier Than 2x***

Exercises for Reflection,
Processing, and Practising the Lessons

BIG ACTION BOOKS

BigActionBooks.com

Contents

Claim your free bonus

There's a free bonus waiting for you as thanks for picking up this workbook. We think you'll like it. Inside, you'll find a list of the most impactful self development books from this year, including:

- Top books for self-growth and mindfulness
- Top books for financial growth
- Top books for relationships (including yourself)
- Top books for productivity and "Getting Things Done"

We hope they provide a little inspiration for you - and perhaps some new discoveries.

To get your free bonus, scan the QR code below or visit BigActionBooks.com/bonus.

Scan to get your free bonus

Introduction

Learn how to 10x your results - and achieve more by doing less - from some of the world's leading minds in entrepreneurship and personal growth.

WHY THIS WORKBOOK?
You've read Dan Sullivan & Benjamin Hardy's fabulous book about how to achieve extraordinary results in both life and business by doing less - with more focus on the important things. Now it's time to actually *practice* it - write; journal; put the lessons in motion.

This workbook was created as a **companion** to Dan Sullivan & Benjamin Hardy's "*10x Is Easier Than 2x*". While reading the book, we found ourselves wishing for a place where we could write, process and practise the book's exercises in a constructive, concise way. The lessons in the book are excellent - but there isn't much space to actually write in the book itself. Instead, we found ourselves cobbling notes together in various places - notebooks, journals, pieces of paper - all of which would eventually get lost, or at the very least, not be helpful in putting the lessons into practice. That's how this workbook was born.

HOW TO USE THIS WORKBOOK
This workbook is like a faithful friend to *10x Is Easier Than 2x* . You'll find exactly what's advertised: dozens of exercises based on the book, summarised and formatted, with space to answer.

- Exercises based on the book's teachings - extracted into one single place
- Space to write under each exercise
- Lists, ruled lines and space for you to answer, journal and reflect
- Clearly organised and well-formatted so it's easy to follow

In each section, we've extracted the main premise of the exercise, and then added space to respond and practise the lessons. This may come in the format of a table to fill in, space to free-write, or other exercises. You'll also notice the "Parts" and "Chapters" referenced in the book, so you can easily find the section if you need to look back on it for further context.

If you want to not only *read about* how to 10x your results while actually doing less - but also put the lessons into practice - this workbook, as well as your own dedication, will help you do just that.

Enjoy, and thank you.
Let's dive in!

Please note: This is an unofficial workbook companion for 10x Is Easier Than 2x to help motivated do-ers process the lessons from this fantastic book. It is not created by or associated with the authors in any official way.

Chapter 1: The Surprising Simplicity of 10x Growth

Mindset and Results

The authors begin the book by stressing that high performers achieve **more** by **doing less.** Partly, that's because they focus on what truly matters, prioritising quality over quantity.

As they suggest, the path to achieving big results is to make your goals impossible. There are two steps to this process:

1. Specify your goals.
2. Make your goals bigger, even impossible.

The trick behind this is that going for 10x goals will help you land near 2x results at the very least. On the other hand, going for 2x goals will only keep you trapped in taking the same actions again and again.

It is important to keep in mind that the goal determines the process. If you go after an impossible goal, chances are that you are not going to achieve it by doing what you are **currently** doing.

> **Note:** Throughout this workbook, you'll see examples in some places, listed in *grey handwriting like this.* These are just to give you an idea of the kind of action points you might like to take - but feel free to use or ignore them as best suits your style. There's also a section at the back of this notebook for free-form notes and journaling.

Example text

Let's break this exercise down into two parts. Move on to the next page for part one.

Take some time to think of your current goals, or goals that you are considering pursuing, and write them down in the spaces below. You can describe them in as much detail as you like.

Example: Make $5,000 in additional income next month.

Example: Get 10 new paying clients by the end of this quarter.

Now that you have specified your goals, rewrite them - but this time, we ask you to write them with a **10x perspective**. Go really crazy and free, push these goals to the limits without judging yourself or your current situation.

Example: Make $50,000 in additional income next month.

Example: Get 100 new paying clients by the end of this quarter.

10x VS 2x Framework

To help yourself make the leap to the next level, you will need to understand, **at a deep level,** which actions bring the desired results and focus on those.

The authors connect the 10x principle to the Pareto principle.

Pareto's Law:

- Nearly 20% of what you do brings 80% of results.
- Nearly 80% of what you do brings 20% of results.

By applying the 10x principle to your life and goals, you will be forced to figure out which 20% matters most to you and your goals. If you operate with a goal of 2x, you will likely get stuck doing the 80% that doesn't produce results, over and over.

Let's begin this exercise by identifying one of your goals and then applying the 80/20 rule to it. You can choose whichever goal of yours you like.

My Goal

What actions am I taking right now to reach this goal?

Which of these actions actually produce 80% of my results?

*What **new** actions could I take to help generate higher quality results?*

Making 10x Jumps

Good things start happening to people when they commit to something with all their power. However, there is always a risk of getting trapped in the 80% 'junk' actions that don't help the final result.

We need to get rid of that junk because only then you will be free to focus on what truly matters, and maximise your results.

There are two questions you can ask yourself:

1. Who can help me get rid of the 80% junk?
2. How can ***I*** get rid of the 80% junk?

Let's dive right in and work on the first question. Who can help you get rid of your 80% junk? Recall the authors' example from the book, where they talk about a female real estate agent who elevated her game by hiring an assistant to delegate her 80% percent to.

Then, she was able to elevate her business by doing the 20% that mattered and she was able to jump to the next level.

In your case, WHO can help take care of your 80% junk? Aim for at least 3 ideas here.

Next, let's ask HOW. Is there a way <u>**you**</u> can automate or remove your 80% percent without external assistance? Maybe there is, or maybe not.

Keep in mind that the WHO question is probably more important than the HOW question, but with technology available today, there is a possibility you can automate things. And don't forget the power of 'addition by subtraction' - some things might be possible to simply <u>remove</u> without a big impact on your results.

Your turn. What are some ways you can automate or remove your 80% junk?

Chapter 2: 10x The Quality of Everything You Do

Shed Your 2x Identity

The authors begin this chapter by telling the story of Chad, a young man who was fresh out of college and managed to find a job in an investment firm.

Although his managers wanted him to manage the funds of several clients, Chad was avoiding that, clarifying that he only wanted to manage clients with a minimum amount of $100,000.

Chad spent much of his time studying and acquiring certifications that would elevate his game. Although it took some time, he got his first big client by playing by his own rules. Many more followed after that, increasing in net worth.

A few years later, Chad built his own firm by constantly adhering to what he believed his standards should be. By focusing more on quality, he could focus less on quantity. We all consciously know that we have to stay true to our standards, and indeed strive to adopt higher standards, but how many of us actually do it?

How many of us eliminate what's not a part of the 10x principle?

As the authors suggest, when you commit to a specific standard far above your current capability and confidence, it pushes you outside your knowledge and comfort zone, prompting you to act with courage.

This exercise will ask you 4 tough questions. Take some time to reflect on them and answer them honestly, going into as much detail as you like.

What are the standards you hold for yourself? These could be general standards, or related to a specific goal (or set of goals) you're currently working towards.

Did you consciously choose these standards, or did you adopt them based on outside influences?

What is likely to happen if you dramatically elevated your standards?

What 80% would have to be removed, in order to elevate your standards?

10x The Quality of What You Do

The authors discuss the story of a famous Youtuber going by the nickname MrBeast. Jimmy Donaldson, as his real name is, was interviewed in a podcast and he revealed the secret of his success.

As he said, it is easier to focus on one thing and produce better quality than focusing on 2 or more things. Practically, the more time you can attribute to one thing, the better you can get at it. Consequently, you increase the quality of its production.

Jimmy gave an example from his own world, saying that having a specialist video editor who can only focus on that, opens more opportunities for him to focus on other elements of his videos. Jimmy can't spend 10 hours focusing on the video editing process but the video editor can.

Now it's your turn to ask yourself two important questions. First, take some time to write down some of the activities/tasks you are doing in your life, choosing those that either dictate your life or are perceived as 'necessary'.

Next, answer the questions below to dig deeper into your current focus.

Are you focused primarily on quality or volume?

Are you doing five or more different jobs, or do you have a growing team of people handling your 80%?

10x Often and Become the Best

The authors provide yet another example, that of the author and entrepreneur James Clear, writer of Atomic Habits.

James Clear had set up 4 businesses and various smaller projects before deciding that he wanted to make a transition from a blog writer to a book writer. Two of his businesses were successful and running on auto-pilot after he had gone 10x on them.

James knew that if he applied the same 10x rule to his new goal, he would be able to achieve it. Having found the people that can handle his 80% for him, James focused on writing his book and wrote Atomic Habits, which became a best-seller.

James Clear talks about two important rules:

1. You need to eliminate distractions.
2. Behavior is a reflection of your identity.

In other words, adopting a 10x attitude really comes from **within**. Therefore, it is important to also **behave** 10x, not only write down 10x goals.

Once you habitually behave and think 10x, you start applying the rule to every aspect of your life, including relationships, fitness, finance, or whatever else you like.

Use the following prompts to do some introspection based on James Clear's advice.

In your own life, what are some distractions you can eliminate today?

What kind of behaviors you can adopt today to become a 10x performer?

- *How should you act?*
- *How should you conduct yourself in the situations and environments you find yourself in?*

Chapter 3: 10x Embraces Abundance and Rejects Scarcity

Escape Scarcity and Embrace Wanting

The authors differentiate between **needing** and **wanting**. They connect needing to scarcity, and wanting to expansion or creation.

More specifically:

Needing:

- Scarcity.
- You feel like you should justify your needs.
- They often come from others.

Wanting:

- Love and creation.
- No need to justify your wants. You should not.
- Comes purely from within. You are attracted to it.

To clarify further, the authors outline some more differences between the two:

1. Needing is extrinsically motivated, whereas wanting is intrinsically motivated.
2. Needing is security-driven, whereas wanting is freedom-driven.
3. Needing is scarcity-minded, whereas wanting is abundance-minded.
4. Needing is reactive, whereas wanting is creative.

If we strictly commit to what we want, we can gradually earn **freedom**.

There are two core types of freedom according to the authors:

1. **Freedom from**: Externally escaping from what you don't want - this is avoidance-motivated.
2. **Freedom to**: Internally committing to, and courageously choosing, what you most want - this is approach-motivated.

Now it's your turn to reflect on the above:

Are you a needer or a wanter? Why?

If you are fully honest with yourself, what are the things that you truly want? Use the space to reflect below (this may include various aspects of your life such as business, money, relationships, fitness and so-on, which is why we've included quite a lot of space).

Define Your Unique Ability

Recall P-Rod's example from the book, a skateboarder who has released multiple signature shoes with Nike, placing himself in a list with names such as Michael Jordan, Kobe Bryant, and Lebron James.

P-Rod believed in his **Unique Ability** and has always used it. We all carry different Unique Abilities but they all have something in common: We can use them to provide value and create wealth.

Your Unique Ability gives you a sense of purpose, it is something that keeps surfacing inside of you.

Let's try to identify your own Unique Ability.

What is the unique value you provide to others, that no one else can? What things about you are truly 'you', that no-one else has? Think about both what you value as unique in yourself, and, if it helps, what other people say is unique about you (you can also ask close friends or family about this). Take your time and answer below.

Having a better idea of what your Unique Ability is, let's move on to how to harness it.

What's the 80% of your life keeping you busy but unproductive, because it's keeping you outside your Unique Ability?

In order to further distill and understand your Unique Ability, there are 5 specific requirements you need to fill:

1. Honesty with yourself
2. Expanding your vision
3. Imagining your ideal future self
4. Clarifying your 20%
5. Ridding yourself of the 80%

Since we have already covered most of these items, let's focus on number 3 from the list above.

How do you imagine your ideal future self? How do you act? How do you talk? What projects are you working on? Are you loyal to your wants? Are you going after freedom? Write as many details as possible, always keeping the 10x rule in mind.

Sellers and Buyers

In every situation, a person can be either a **seller** or a **buyer**. Whichever role you assume, this affects how your interactions with other people turn out.

The difference between the two is that a buyer can walk away. On the other hand, the seller is a pleaser, who fights to retain attention and keep the other person from leaving. Being a seller puts you at a disadvantage.

Even when you are practically a seller in real life, you should behave like a buyer. The buyer knows what they want and they have specific standards. You should do the same thing when you are a seller.

In your own life, what are some situations where you can stop behaving like a seller and adopt the buyer persona/mentality?

Chapter 4: Uncover Your 10x Past to Clarify Your 10x Future

The Gap and the Gain

The authors introduce us to a unique concept they call "**The Gap and the Gain**". Both of them refer to states of mentality.

Beginning with the Gap, it means that you live in a state of being where **you compare what is to what should be**. This concept can be applied to the smallest of things, such as not appreciating the food your mother has cooked for you, to the biggest of things, like feeling useless because you don't have as nice a body as the fitness instructor you saw on your Social Media feed.

An example mentioned by the authors is Mathew Perry, the famous actor who has admitted that he went after women, drugs, and alcohol in order to fill a huge internal Gap.

On the other hand, the Gain is a state of being where **you measure yourself against yourself**. More specifically, the authors suggest that you need to compare yourself backwards because this is the only way to realize the progress you've made.

To measure your Gains, you can use several perspectives and timeframes. This exercise will h elp you remember how great you are, and that you have probably made some real progress, even if it doesn't always feel that way.

Move to next page to get started - we'll start from longer ago, and move to more recently, in that order. Here we go →

How have you grown as a person over the past three years?

What are the biggest things you've learned or accomplished in the past 12 months?

How are you clearer on your goals and vision than you were 90 days ago?

In what ways is your life different and better than it was 30 days ago?

What important progress have you made in the past seven days?

What progress have you made in the past 24 hours?

Review Your 10x Jumps

There is no doubt that you have made 10x jumps in the past. Now that you are familiar with the concept, it will be easier for you to identify those jumps.

In addition, you will be challenged to discover the 20% of those jumps. In other words, you will be challenged to recall what you did right.

To begin with, identify **five** of your past 10x jumps and write them below.

1. ______________________________

   ____

2. ______________________________

   ____

3. ______________________________

   ____

4. ______________________________

   ____

5. ______________________________

   ____

To add some simplicity to this process, give each of your previous 10x jumps a name and a timeline. An example the authors use in the book:

"Getting married and into a Ph.D. program (2011-2014)"

Your turn - name each of your previous jumps in a similar way:

1. ____________________

2. ____________________

3. ____________________

4. ____________________

5. ____________________

Lastly, note the **20%** of each 10x jump, as well as the **80%** that you let go of at each level. As you reflect on the 20% of each 10x jump you've made, reflect on how that 20% helped you further develop your **Unique Ability**. Space to expand below.

1. The 20% for this jump was:

   ____

   ____

   ____

   The 80% I let go of was:

   ____

   ____

   ____

   The impact on my Unique Ability was:

   ____

   ____

   ____

2. The 20% for this jump was:

The 80% I let go of was:

The impact on my Unique Ability was:

3. The 20% for this jump was:

The 80% I let go of was:

The impact on my Unique Ability was:

4. The 20% for this jump was:

The 80% I let go of was:

The impact on my Unique Ability was:

5. The 20% for this jump was:

The 80% I let go of was:

The impact on my Unique Ability was:

Define Your Fitness Function

A **Fitness Function** is a term used by the authors to describe the process of refining your standards and figuring out how you should act in order to live up to them.

Defining your Fitness Function is a matter of where you keep your focus. The authors outline 4 specific laws when it comes to focus:

1. Whatever you focus on expands.
2. Whatever you focus on, you create more of.
3. Whatever you focus on, you become.
4. Whatever you focus on, you develop a finer and more specific understanding of.

Why is all of this important? Because the authors have written their book keeping in mind that a noble purpose to have in life is achieving **mastery of your Unique Ability**. That's why they like to ask many questions about the process of refining your goals, vision, standards, etc.

Next up, we invite you to answer a series of questions that will help you further refine your standards in order to optimize your default behaviors and take your life to the next level.

What do you ultimately want to be and do? What standards do you want to create and realize?

What minimum standards - such as the level of client you work with or the time it takes to run a marathon - will help you adapt and evolve to where you want to be?

What are the results you want to be able to produce and master?

Writing Yourself a Dream Check

The authors begin this section by referring to Jim Carrey's famous story. As Jim Carrey has said, there was a time when he decided to write himself a check.

Of course, that check had no real value but it was used by him to remind him of the value he can offer, which can always be traded with wealth.

Jim Carrey managed to become one of the most iconic figures of cinema, so there is no wonder he earned the amount he had written on the check: 10 million dollars.

Writing yourself a Dream Check is a way to gamify your reality and tell your subconscious mind that this is what you are worth.

Take a few moments to define your own Dream Check below. This might be related to a large project you're working on, a business, or related to your Unique Ability. Go for it:

Now, move to the next page and ask yourself an important question. Try to really reflect on it and write some answers with depth.

What value do I need to provide and how can my Unique Ability be so valuable that someone will pay me my Dream Check?

Chapter 5: Take 150+ Free Days Per Year

Free Days

The authors discuss the story of a man named Dan, who is an actor who came to the conclusion that days can be categorised into three types:

1. Practice days.
2. Performance days.
3. Rejuvenation/recovery days.

Practice days are also called **Buffer Days** by the authors. Here is where the preparation happens. For an actor, it would be learning their lines or doing rehearsal. For an athlete would be going to practice or training.

Performance days are called **Focus Days** by the authors. This is where the actual event happens. An actor performs their play in front of an audience, an athlete plays their game against a rival team, an employee goes to the office to do the work.

Lastly, Rejuvenation (recovery) Days are also called **Free Days** by the authors because they are all about recovery and rest.

Now take a moment to figure out what kind of a day you had today. Tick the appropriate box below. Note that Focus days and Buffer days can also be squeezed into the same day.

Today was a:

- ☐ Buffer Day
- ☐ Focus Day
- ☐ Free Day

Free Days

Recovery and rest should be the main focus of these days. The authors refer to the NBA player Lebron James, who invests large sums of money on his recovery.

Why would he do that? Because high performers know that rest works like a slingshot. It pulls you slightly back only to launch you further forward.

Resting boosts your productivity and helps you take your game to the next level. There is no human being that can excel without recovery and rest.

Resting does not just refer to the body, but to the mind as well. The authors suggest that we all should learn how to **psychologically detach from work**.

Another source of motivation to be absent from work sometimes would be to test your team. If you have a team working for you and you are not there to support them, you will be able to notice how they function without you and make some honest assessments.

Let's begin this exercise by writing down the Free (recovery) Days you will have this month. Write the exact days in the spaces below.

Next write down some activities you can do on your rest days (or not do), to enhance your recovery.

Focus and Buffer Days

The authors group these two types of days together because the reality for many people is they can't separate them.

Imagine you are an employee or a small business owner/manager. You can rarely take a day just to concentrate on improving the processes and systems of your business/work. That would be a Buffer Day.

For many of us who work 9-to-5 jobs or other similar job models, it is simply impossible to separate Focus from Buffer days.

Knowing this, the authors offer a couple of suggestions for both the Focus and Buffer parts of the day:

Focus:

- Focus on the 20% that matters.
- Schedule big blocks of time and space for uninterrupted deep work.
- Don't take on more than 3 important goals per day.

Buffer:

- When done working, unplug completely and recover.
- Put your phone on Airplane Mode 30-60 minutes before sleeping.
- Before you go to sleep, write down 3 wins you achieved today.

Take a moment to read the above pointers again and then move to the next page to schedule your next day according to those pointers. If you can't totally incorporate them, get as close as possible.

My Day Tomorrow

Chapter 6: Build A Self-Managing Company

Level 1 to Level 2 Entrepreneurship: From Rugged Individual to Leader Applying 'Who, Not How'

The authors suggest there are 4 levels you have to reach as a businessperson in order to build a self-managing company.

The very first step is to jump from Level 1 to Level 2 entrepreneurship by transforming from a rugged individual to a leader who applies the concept of WHO.

Recall Tim's story from the book, a business owner who didn't see any significant progress in his business for the first decade. However, the next decade was very different and he made a 10x jump.

There were some specific attributes that Tim incorporated into his progress. Those were:

1. **The Story**: Your organization or business needs a powerful origin story.
2. **An Ideology**: In Tim's own words "There needs to be a mission and purpose in your organization that gives people goose bumps". Timeless ideologies are based on principles.
3. **A Symbol**: The business needs a strong-sounding and clear name, as well as a symbol or logo people can associate with, like the Nike swoosh symbol.
4. **Shared Rituals**: A ritual can be any activity that is unique and consistent, which triggers a sense of meaning and belonging. These rituals strengthen the individual's commitment to the business and its ideology.
5. **The Enemy**: Interestingly, it's often easier for people to bond about what they don't like, than what they do. This enables you to clearly point to something and say, "That's not us."
6. **The Language**: Every sticky organization has a shared insider language, with unique words, acronyms, and shared meanings which are continually used in conversation and presented in education materials.
7. **The Leader**: Every business or movement has a leader. This leader is seen as an attractive character and a servant.

The authors have distilled some transformational Leadership principles from Tim's insights that you can use to elevate your business and team:

1. **Idealised Influence**: Transformational leaders are role models who, through their actions and values, inspire those who follow them. They take risks and display convictions that create a sense of confidence in those they lead.

2. **Inspirational Motivation**: Transformational leaders inspire a sense of purpose in those they lead. They communicate with clarity and shift seemingly negative or challenging circumstances into opportunities for gains.

3. **Intellectual Stimulation**: Transformational leaders value creativity and autonomy among each team member. The leader involves members in the decision-making process and stimulates creative thinking.

4. **Individualised Consideration**: Transformational leaders know that each member of the team is a unique individual, with unique goals and a Unique Ability.

With all of that said, it is your turn to take action and start building your team.

Move to the next page to decide who is going to be your first WHO, when you are going to acquire them, how you are going to acquire them, and what responsibilities you will delegate to them.

WHO, when, how, and their responsibilities:

Level 2 to Level 3 Entrepreneurship: From Leader Applying 'Who Not How', to 'Self-Managing Company'

The authors begin by outlining the importance of mutual trust. To become a trusted leader, you have to trust others first. In reality, that is the only way to create a self-managing company.

Trusting others motivates them intrinsically to do better. The more you trust them, the more they will do for you. Ultimately, it's all about giving your team freedom.

There are 3 levels of intrinsic motivation:

1. Autonomy: You have freedom to do what you want, how you want, when you want, and with whom you want.
2. Mastery: You have the freedom to continually elevate and evolve the artistry and skill of your Unique Ability.
3. Relatedness: You have the freedom to create transformational relationships with the 10x individuals you want to collaborate and transform with.

Now it's time to ask yourself some questions. Answer honestly and see how you can move to the next level.

Are you a rugged individualist or are you a leader applying 'Who Not How'?

Do you trust your Whos or do you only trust yourself?

Imagine what it would be and feel like to have a Self-Managing Company, where you've freed yourself up to explore, expand, innovate, learn, and create. What would this be like or you?

Are you ready to become a transformational leader? Which parts of you answer 'yes', and which parts answer 'no'? For those that answer 'no', why is this, and what can you do to overcome it?

Level 3 to Level 4 Entrepreneurship: From 'Self-Managing Company' to 'Self-Expanding Unique Ability Teamwork'

This is the point where you help your Whos focus on ***their own 20%***. One of the authors talks about their own secretary. For two whole years, she was doing a great job managing his 80% but she lost the ball when the author started throwing more and more at her.

Then, the author realised that he was not giving her space to focus on her own Unique Ability, so he prompted her to find another assistant that would manage her 80%, so his first WHO would focus on her 20%.

To follow the same philosophy, ask yourself the following questions and reply honestly. Try to figure out what steps you need to take to reach your final level.

Do you lead by example and create a culture of freedom, where those in your team are given permission to take ***their*** *Unique Ability seriously as well?*

Does your self-managing team have the confidence to go all-in on their Unique Ability, honing their own roles and bringing on additional 'Whos' to handle their former 80%?

Would it be a good idea to hire more WHOs in other areas of your life apart from business/career? What would those areas be and what kinds of people do you need?

You made it!

You've completed the workbook.

Claim your free bonus

There's a free bonus waiting for you as thanks for picking up this workbook. We think you'll like it. Inside, you'll find a list of the most impactful self development books from this year, including:

- Top books for self-growth and mindfulness
- Top books for financial growth
- Top books for relationships (including yourself)
- Top books for productivity and "Getting Things Done"

We hope they provide a little inspiration for you - and perhaps some new discoveries.

To get your free bonus, scan the QR code below or visit BigActionBooks.com/bonus.

Scan to get your free bonus

Would you help us with a review?

If you enjoyed the workbook, we'd be so grateful you could help us out by leaving a review on Amazon (even a super short one!). Reviews help us so much - in spreading the word, in helping others decide if the workbook is right for them, and as feedback for our team.

If you'd like to give us any suggestions, need help with something, or to find more workbooks for other self-development books, please visit us at BigActionBooks.com.

Thank you

Thank you so much for picking up the Workbook for Dan Sullivan & Benjamin Hardy's *10x Is Easier Than 2x*. We really hope you enjoyed it, and that it helped you practise the lessons in everyday life.

Thanks again,
The Big Action Books team

BIG ACTION BOOKS

BigActionBooks.com

Notes

Notes

Notes

Notes

Notes

Notes

Notes

Made in the USA
Las Vegas, NV
28 November 2024

12834641R00037